TEXAS RANGERS

BILL SHAW

CREATIVE EDUCATION

Mickey Rivers slides for home. The former Yankee has been one of the main spark plugs for the modern-day Rangers.

ISBN 0-87191-876-5

TEXAS RANGERS

Hold onto your cap! The story of the Texas Rangers is the story of some firsts, some lasts and some nevers. It's the story of a team that wants to be the greatest in baseball — and just might pull it off.

The Texas Rangers have only been in the American League since 1972. Before that they were known as the Washington Senators. Their home was Washington D.C., the capital of the United States where they played stirring baseball for 71 years before moving to Texas and changing their name.

Why did they move? Well, towards the end of the 1960s and the early 70s, the fans in Washington D.C. just weren't turning out to watch the Senators anymore. It was a sad time for baseball fans everywhere. Here was a team that had been around since the American League was formed, way back in the early 1900's—and it was a shame to see that tradition disappear.

The Senators played in three World Series in the early years. Then after winning the American League pennant in 1933, they lost their luster. Year after year, the losses

Ferguson Jenkins fired a one-hitter in this 1974 contest with the Oakland Athletics. Fergie came to Texas from the Cubs.

THE BABE'S BIG BOOMER Babe Ruth's record breaking 60th home run in the 1927 season was hit against the Washington Senators. Washington pitcher Tom Zachary threw a screwball to the Babe in the eighth inning with the score tied 2-2. The Babe missed the first pitch but hit the second one and knocked it deep into right field for his 60th home run.

SEVENTH INNING STRETCH
William Howard Taft, the president of the United States, was attending a Senators game on a hot afternoon. He was a huge man and in the seventh inning he stood up to stretch his legs. The other fans in the park stood up and stretched too. Ever since that day, fans take a stretch in the middle of the seventh inning.

mounted up. Slowly but surely, the fans lost interest and drifted away.

In 1971 Senators' owner Robert Short made a startling announcement. He was moving the team to Arlington, Texas, just outside of Dallas. Maybe with a new name in a new place, the team would improve and the fans would fill the ballpark once again.

The fans in Arlington were thrilled. Swiftly, they went to work on tiny 10,000-seat Arlington Stadium. The hammers and saws sang out. Soon, Arlington Stadium was ready. Now it would seat more than 35,000 eager fans.

One of the greatest legends in baseball history — Hall-of-Famer Ted Williams — managed the first Ranger team in 1972. When the smoke had cleared, the new team found itself deep in the American League cellar, 38½ games out of first place.

Williams retired from managing after that first season in Texas, and Whitey Herzog took over. Whitey lasted a

Veteran spitball pitcher Gaylord Perry warms up at 1977 spring training camp at Pompano Beach, Florida.

year. In all, the Rangers had 10 different managers in their first 10 years in Arlington.

During that same ten years, however, some of baseball's most talented hitters and pitchers played for them.

Pitchers? How about Ferguson Jenkins, Gaylord Perry, Bert Blyleven, Jim Bibby and Denny McClain, just to name a few.

And some great hitters, too. Former Yankee Mickey Rivers found a happy new home with the Rangers. In 1980 Mickey hammered out a .333 batting average, the best in Rangers history. Mickey doesn't stand alone, though. Guys like Al Oliver, Bert Campaneris, Willie Horton and Bobby Bonds have brought some big bats to the Rangers, too.

One of baseball's best managers, hot-tempered and hard driving Billy Martin, guided the Rangers for two big seasons. In 1974 he brought "Billy Ball" to Arlington and managed the Rangers to a second place finish, their best season ever in Texas. Martin stayed through the 1974 season and captained the team to a third place finish.

Setting his sights. Bert Blyleven kicks and readies in 1976 game action against the Yanks.

BATTING .500 Frank Howard, who played with the Rangers in 1972, had 10 home runs in 20 times at bat with the Washington Senators in 1968.

Rangers fans remember all the games that were lost by one measly run that year. With a few more breaks, it could've been a championship year for Billy and the gang.

Although they haven't been in Texas very long, the franchise has a long and colorful history, going way back to the beginning of the American League when they were known as the Washington Senators.

Let's take a look at the proud old team, long before they became the Texas Rangers we know today.

LOOKING BACK AT THE SENATORS

It's impossible to talk about the great old days of the Senators without taking a long look at the great Walter Johnson, one of the top five pitchers who ever lived. The colorful Hall-of-Famer pitched for the Senators for over 20 seasons, taking them to the World Series and setting baseball records that may never be broken.

Double play! Bert Campaneris balances on one leg after firing the second out in this 1977 double-play. Campy helped the Rangers to a solid second-place finish that year.

Walter joined the Senators in 1907, a few years before WWI. He struggled for the first couple years, learning to control his blazing fastball, and mastering a big sweeping curve that would later confuse batters throughout the league.

And then — listen to this — from 1910 through 1917 Johnson never won less than 25 games each season. No pitcher since then has ever come close to matching that record.

Johnson was truly an amazing athlete. Baseball historians say he was the fastest pitcher who ever lived. Faster than Nolan Ryan, Sandy Koufax or Lefty Grove. Back in those days there were no radar guns to time a pitcher's speed, but those who saw Walter overpower the game's greatest hitters have no doubts about his speed. Awesome is the only word to describe it.

"How do they know what Johnson's got," asked one amused sportswriter in 1912, "nobody's seen it yet."

Johnson's power and speed were so impressive the

Safe at home. Juan Beniquez scores on a single by Bump Wills in the late innings of a '77 heart-stopper against the A's.

players nicknamed him "The Big Train", after the big powerful locomotives of the day.

It's a rare pitcher who wins 300 games in a career, but Johnson won 416 games, losing only 279. His records sparked the Senators during those early years. In 1913, his record was 36-7. He fanned 3,508 batters in his career. He pitched in 802 games. Twelve times he led the American League in strikeouts. His pitching achievements are endless and would require another book just to list them all.

The Senators first American League pennant in 1924 came largely as a result of Johnson's great pitching. His 23-7 record, according to Senators Manager Bucky Harris, was the secret to the Senators' great season.

Stories about "The Big Train" are endless. Once he was pitching against the Detroit Tigers and the bases were full. The Senators were in big trouble. The next three hitters were the great Ty Cobb, Sam Crawford and Bobby Veach. The Big Train threw nine smoking fast-

Ranger spirit. Power-hitter Richie Zisk trots towards teammates Sandy Alomar and Dave May. Zisk had just brought them home with a three-run homer.

16

balls and whiffed all three batters. Nine pitches, nine strikes. The fans sat spellbound.

Another time he struck out four hitters in one inning. That's right. Four in one inning. How? One of the hitters reached first base on a dropped third strike that skittered away from the catcher. The Big Train just mowed down the next three hitters. Four strikeouts in one single inning.

Though Johnson was a great pitcher, he didn't do so well as a manager. He skippered the Senators from 1929-32, but they never finished very high in the standings. Maybe because The Big Train wasn't out there pitching anymore.

He left the Senators and managed the Cleveland Indians in 1934 and 1935. The next year — 1936 — he was elected to the Baseball Hall of Fame. Sadly, he died of a brain tumor at age 59. Today, the name of Walter Perry Johnson, The Big Train, is still whispered with reverence whenever baseball historians speak of the great all-time hurler.

Under the leadership of manager Pat Corralles, the Rangers struggled through disappointing seasons in 1979 and '80.

THE DAY THE FANS STAYED HOME
Very few hotdogs were sold when the Rangers played the California Angels on September 21, 1973. Only 2,513 fans showed up. It was the smallest crowd in Arlington Stadium history.

WHAT A SERIES!

Despite the brilliant pitching of Walter Johnson, the Washington Senators didn't win their first pennant until 1924. What a year that was! It was Bucky Harris' first season managing the club, and he took them right to the top.

They called Bucky the "Boy Manager" because he was only 29-years-old when he took command of the struggling club. He was still a player, too. Back then, lots of managers were actually player/managers. Bucky managed the squad from his slot at second base. In the great 1924 World Series against John McGraw's powerful New York Giants, Bucky batted .333, leading the team to its first series championship.

It was also the first World Series appearance for Walter Johnson, the rugged veteran. It was his 18th season with the Senators. Time was running short for Walter. Through the entire 1924 season, his ancient arm had done wonders for the team. He had won 23 games and

Texas Rangers second baseman Kurt Bevacqua goes airborne to stop Yankee Mickey Rivers' lunge for second. Mickey would soon be traded to the Rangers.

led the league in earned-run average, strikeouts and shutouts.

No wonder the entire nation was pulling for Johnson to reach down deep and continue pitching right through the Series. In the first game, however, the big bats of the Giants peppered Johnson for 14 hits to defeat the Senators, 4-3. Washington ace southpaw Tom Zachary shut out the Giants in the second and sixth games. In that sixth game it was player/manager Bucky Harris who drove in the two winning runs.

In the fifth game the Giants did it again to the Big Train, shelling him for 13 hits and easily defeating the Senators, 6-2. It seemed the big right-hander was no match for the hard-hitting Giants of the National League.

The Series had come down to a seventh and deciding game.

Right-handed hurler Curly Ogden started for the Senators. The game was tied 3-3 in the eighth when Bucky brought in Fred Marberry to relieve on the mound. Marberry was stale that day. He stayed just one inning

BIG THIEF WILLS
Heading into the 1982 season, Bump Wills was the Rangers all-time "prince of pilfer" with 161 stolen bases.

Headed for Texas. Oakland pitcher Don Stanhouse packs his bag after it was announced that he was traded to a new team in Texas called the Rangers. (1972)

before another reliever — a guy called Big Train — was called to the mound to save the day.

Johnson pitched brilliantly, handcuffing the Giants hitters and hurling his way to a dramatic 4-3 win in 12 innings. Walter Johnson and the Senators had pulled off the cliffhanger of the decade. The Series was theirs. In our nation's capital, the fans danced in the streets.

In 1925 the Senators won the American League pennant again. This time, however, the World Series results would be a little different.

TWO IN A ROW

There was a new kind of excitement in Washington D.C. It was hard to believe, but true. The fans rejoiced. Their beloved Senators were playing in their second World Series in a row. Could they pull off another victory? It wouldn't be easy. The opposition was none other than the Pittsburgh Pirates, a team that was known for scrapping to the finish.

For the first time in a World Series a team actually

came back to win the championship after losing the first three games. Here's what happened: The Pirates lost the first three and it looked for sure like the Senators would easily win their second World Series in a row. In fact, the Pirates were never ahead in the Series until the eighth inning of the seventh game. Then they smashed across three runs against The Big Train on a muddy, fog-bound field with Washington shortstop Roger Peckinpaugh making three costly errors.

The outcome? The Pirates won the final game, 9-7, and snatched the World Series victory from the bewildered Senators.

That loss seemed to take the wind out of the Senators' sails. They went into a nosedive after the great 1924-25 seasons. Somehow, nothing seemed to work for them. Bucky Harris stayed until the end of the 1928 season when he was traded to Detroit for Jack Warner. But Bucky and the Senators would be back together again for eight more seasons beginning in 1934 when he returned to manage the club.

C'mere. Shortstop Roy Smalley had one of those days in this 1976 contest against the Cleveland Indians. The Rangers were beaten, 9-1 with 12 hits.

SUNDBERG'S RECORDS
Jim Sundberg makes the Rangers' all-time top ten in eight different categories, including most games played by a Ranger (1,128); most at bats (3,598); most hits, runs, doubles and triples.

27

HOW WILLIE HORTON GOT SIGNED

When he was a 16-year-old high school baseball player, Willie Horton's team played a game in Tiger Stadium in Detroit, Michigan. Willie, who was only a junior in high school, slugged a home run into the upper deck, something few major league hitters can do. Willie, a future Ranger, was signed to a pro baseball contract as soon as he finished high school.

1933 WORLD SERIES

For the New York Giants it was their 10th World Series. The Senators were in their third. It took just five games for the Giants to smother the Senators. The Big Train had retired and without him the Senators seemed lifeless through the short series.

Player-manager Joe Cronin seemed unable to turn the tide for the Senators. They had their moments, but nothing seemed to go their way. Talk about bad luck — when Giant Met Ott pounded a low line drive into left centerfield, the Senators' Fred Schulte raced toward the outfield seats, leaped for the ball and touched it with the tip of his glove. When Umpire Cy Pfirman ruled it a double, the Giants had a fit. The umpires held a conference. Believe it or not Pfirman changed his mind and it was ruled a home run! Such was the luck of the Senators in that series. Nothing went their way.

That series was significant for all of baseball in one small but interesting way:

In 1975 young Mike Cubbage showed the intensity that would make the sure-handed infielder a favorite with the fans.

28

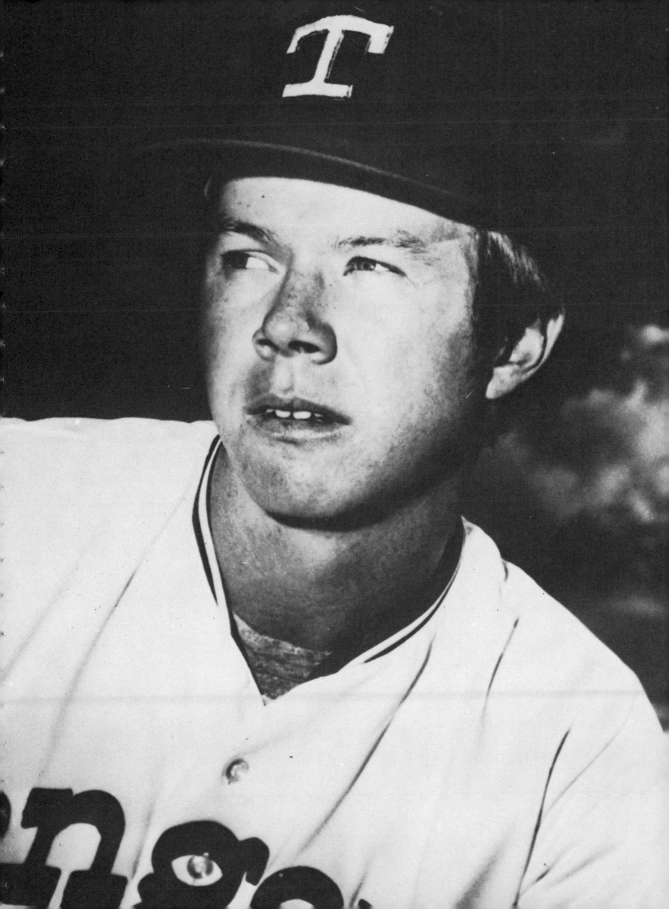

Following the series, the victorious Giants said they would rather have championship rings than watches. For years, the World Series winners had been given watches, but the Giants said they preferred rings. It was the start of a long tradition. World Series champions have received rings ever since then.

MANAGER TED WILLIAMS

After the 1933 season the Senators never quite regained their winning ways. Season after season, they were the team that constantly finished near the bottom of the American League. Players were traded, managers fired, but nothing seemed to work. Fans quit coming to the ballpark and there was talk of moving the team to Texas.

In 1969 Bob Lemon was fired as manager, and the great Hall-of-Famer Ted Williams was hired in his place to guide the struggling baseball team.

Williams, of course, had been one of baseball's leg-

William Amos Sample had the Rangers fans on the edge of their seats when he reeled off a batting streak in 1981.

*STEALING HOME
Toby Harrah did it on May 27, 1972. Buddy Bell did it on June 6, 1981. In between, the Rangers did it 10 more times. Stealing home is the most dangerous play in baseball, and the Rangers are experts at it.*

RANGER ROOKIE
First baseman Mike Hargrove — a favorite of the fans — was the only Texas Ranger rookie to ever win the Rookie of the Year award in the American League.

endary hitters during his playing days with the Boston Red Sox. In 1941 he hit .406 and no one since has come close to hitting that well during a single season. Williams was known as "The Splendid Splinter," because of the tremendous power of his bat. He was a hot-tempered player, quick to anger both on and off the baseball field. He was just a perfectionist and so talented that he sometimes couldn't understand why all players weren't as good as he was.

When Ted took over the Senators in 1969, he had some excellent players on the team. Lee Maye, Ed Stroud, Frank Howard, Sam Bowens and Del Unser to name just a few. Ted's baseball magic worked well that first year as manager. The Senators went from 31 games below. 500 in 1968 to 10 games over .500 in Ted's first year. It was the team's best season in 24 years. They finished just a game out of third place, winning eight of their last nine games. Since Williams had always been such a great hitter, it was no surprise that the '69 Senators used their bats to get their way.

Hometown hero Mike Hargrove of Perryton, Texas looked forward to All-Star action in 1975.

Eddie Brinkman hit .266, Del Unser .286, and Hank Allen .279. Oh yeah, Big Frank Howard hit .296 and boomed out 48 home runs. In the background, Ted was teaching his players how to hit. Mike Epstein, who had always been a weak hitter, clubbed 30 home runs that year. Attendance at Senators games doubled over the previous year. And to top it off, Ted Williams was named manager of the year in the American League.

Only one problem: The improvement didn't continue. The team slipped into last place in 1970, next to last in 1971 and dead last in 1972 when they became the Texas Rangers.

Williams quit.

One of baseball's hottest pitchers at the time was Denny McClain. He looked like another Big Train. In 1967, while pitching for the Detroit Tigers, he won 31 games. In 1970 he joined the Senators and bad luck struck. In his second start as a Senator he balked home the winning run and the Boston Red Sox beat him. Four days later, McClain was bombed again, this time by his

Popular infielder Jim Fregosi had a lot on his mind as the Rangers entered the 1977 season. It would be a good year.

BAIL 'EM OUT
Veteran Ranger John Charles Ellis has frequently used his bat to bail the Rangers out of trouble. John has a similar occupation during the baseball off-season. He is a bail bondsman in his hometown of New London, Conn.

old team, the Detroit Tigers. Six weeks into the season, he had a 4-6 record, an ERA of 3.99, and had given up 24 walks and 75 hits. It seemed nothing would go right for McClain. The pitcher who looked like he might make everyone forget The Big Train was forgotten himself and retired a few years later.

TEXAS

At the close of the 1971 season, owner Bob Short moved the team to Arlington, Texas, renamed them the Texas Rangers and hoped things would improve.

They moved into Arlington Stadium with its long (383-foot) foul lines and deep (400-foot) centerfield wall.

The Rangers have never won an American League pennant. Their first season was terrible, but after that they began to play some exciting baseball.

Unlike the old Senators, the Texas Rangers were rolling up winning seasons, not always, but most of the time.

Since 1974 the Rangers have never finished lower than

Sweet revenge. Toby Harrah scores off teammate Mike Hargrove's sacrifice fly to defeat the Rangers' old rival, the Cleveland Indians, in 1978.

fourth in the American League standings, quite a change from the old Washington Senators days. They did it by playing exciting baseball. Like in 1981 when Manager Don Zimmer twice ordered his runners to try and steal home, the most daring play in baseball.

Playing against the Yankees on April 19, 1981, Zimmer flashed the signal to Ranger Mario Mendoza, who was on third after clubbing out a triple. The Yankee pitcher fired and Mendoza took off, surprising the Yankees and sliding safely into home. A couple months later Buddy Bell also stole home in a game against the Toronto Blue Jays. Manager Zimmer believed in playing daring baseball and catching the other team by surprise.

The Rangers have one of baseball's best third basemen, Buddy Bell. In 1980 he hit .329, sixth best in the American League, drove in 83 runs and banged out 17 homers. Guys like Buddy Bell were filling Arlington Stadium with excited baseball fans.

Buddy is the son of Gus Bell, a powerful-hitting outfielder who played 15 years in the National League with

MORE THAN ONE GOLDEN GLOVE
The Rangers had two Golden Glove winners on their 1980 team. Catcher Jim Sundberg and third baseman Buddy Bell both won the award for their great fielding.

Player of the year for 1981. Buddy Bell shows the hustle that has made him one of the Rangers' all-time stars. He entered the '82 season with three straight Gold Gloves to his credit.

Pittsburgh, Cincinnati, Milwaukee and New York. Like father, like son.

The Rangers were also lucky enough to have one of the American League's top hitters in outfielder Al Oliver. He joined the Rangers in 1978, and hit over .300 every year. After 13 seasons in the majors, Oliver had a lifetime batting average of .319. He's the only Ranger to ever hit three home runs in one game.

The Rangers got a slow start in 1982, but they now look like they have the potential to be one of the best teams in baseball. Despite criticism from Texas fans, Don Zimmer did put together a team of power hitters and hard-throwing pitchers.

With Pat Putnam at first and Mario Mendoza and Mark Wagner switching off at shortstop, not too many balls squirted through Zimmer's infield.

Each year the Rangers are picked to be in there, scrapping with the American League leaders. One of these years they are going to win it all and bring Arlington, Texas its first pennant.

Doc Medich blanked Boston, Seattle, Toronto and Minnesota in 1981. In 1982, he was back on the mound for more.

With a few breaks along the way, the Rangers could have easily won a pennant in the last few years. It just always seems like the breaks went to the other teams. Listen to this. Four times since 1974 Texas has been a runner-up in its division!

"It seems like we have always done just enough to lose," Catcher Jim Sunberg joked after the team finished second in 1981, just five games out of first place.

Al Oliver, the slugging outfielder, thinks the Rangers might have a bad attitude. After all the tough breaks, they sometimes think of themselves as losers. Too many guys remember the long losing years of the Washington Senators.

In 1982 the Rangers signed three promising young pitchers. Lefthanders Frank Tanana and Jon Matlack throw smoke. Tanana came from the Boston Red Sox. He thinks the Rangers can win if they start thinking of themselves as winners, not losers.

In the last couple years almost all the names and faces on the Rangers have changed. Second baseman Doug

Catcher Jim Sundberg closes the door on Dan Meyer of the Seattle Mariners. Sundberg has anchored the Rangers through thick and thin.

ONE WAY OR THE OTHER...
Rangers slugger Bill Stein was batting against Minnesota Twins hurler Jerry Koosman. Koosman threw a wild pitch past catcher Butch Wynegar who ran back to the screen to pick it up. He threw it back to Koosman but it hit Stein's bat and bounced back to the screen again. Ranger base runner Jim Sundberg trotted home and the Rangers won the game 2-1

*IN HIS FATHER'S FOOTSTEPS...
Ranger second baseman Bump Wills is the son of the great Los Angeles Dodger base stealer Maury Wills. Bump is the only Ranger to ever hit an inside-the-park home run in Arlington Stadium.*

Flynn joined the Rangers from the New York Mets. Larry Parrish came over from the Montreal Expos and will roam the outfield with former Met Lee Mazzilli. The spirit of mighty Mickey Rivers and his big bat are still with the Rangers, though, which means the home runs will keep coming.

The Rangers were looking so good for the 1982 season that *Sport Magazine* picked them to win the American League West Division. Though they started slowly, it was obvious they had talent, but they must learn to play together like a team.

Maybe what they need is another "Big Train" like Walter Johnson. Or another manager like Bucky Harris. In fact, some of the fans liked to call manager Don Zimmer "another Bucky Harris". In his first year as manager of the Rangers, they finished second. That was in 1981. Everyone said Zimmer was one of the best managers in baseball, just what the Rangers needed to get them thinking of winning.

Hooray for Harrah! Toby Harrah (middle) tags Duane Kuiper (No. 18) of the Cleveland Indians in this 1977 battle-royal.

Zimmer almost didn't live long enough to become manager. In 1953 when he was playing for a minor-league team in St. Paul, Minn. he was beaned in the head and severely injured. He bounced back, though. Then in 1956 while Zimmer was playing for the Brooklyn Dodgers, Cincinnati Reds pitcher Hal Jeffcoat hit him in the face with a pitch. Zimmer was tough, both on the field and off. He bounced back again. It's the kind of spirit the modern-day Rangers look for in their players and staff.

It's been a long and colorful history for the present day Rangers and the old Washington Senators. The talk in baseball circles is that the Rangers will one day win it all and regain the old glory they knew back in the early days of the Washington Senators. Rangers fans don't think that will happen, they *know* it will.

Oh, Sparky! Southpaw Sparky Lyle left the Yankees in 1978 to pitch for the Rangers. Here he uncorks a smoker in his first game against the Yanks.

RIVERS AND HIS NICKNAMES No one knows why he does it, but Mickey Rivers makes up nicknames for anyone in sight. Some of his favorites include: "Gozzle-head," "Mailbox Head" and "Squash Head."

Stretching it out at first. Veteran Mickey Rivers joined a new corps of younger players who have high hopes for the Texas Rangers in the 1980's.